A Door to the Forest: Poems

A DOOR TO THE FOREST: POEMS

Jon Swan

Random House
New York

The following poems originally appeared in *The
New Yorker*: "A Tale for the Longhouse,"
"Common Prayer," "Fall," "Father, Father, Son
and Son," "Fortune," "Heaven and Earth," "Idyll,
with Siren," "Metamorphosis," "Netherlands'
Birdscape," "Omen," "The Return." "America: a
Formal Elegy" first appeared in *The Observer*.
"Mab" originally appeared in *The Atlantic
Monthly*. "Inaugural: An Anglo-Saxon Riddle" first
appeared in *Antaeus*.

Library of Congress Cataloging in Publication Data
Swan, Jon.
A door to the forest.
I. Title.
PS3569.W25D6   811'.5'4   78–21793
ISBN 0–394–50502–6
ISBN 0–394–73673–7 pbk.

Manufactured in the United States of America
9 8 7 6 5 4 3 2
First Edition

To Marianne

I am indebted to many people and acknowledge,
with gratitude, the kindness and generosity of
Roy Blount, Jr., and Joan Ackermann-Blount, of
Paul Brodeur, of Pirie and Elizabeth MacDonald,
of Tom Rush, of William Russo, of Donald Ogden
Stewart, Jr., and of Paul and Drenka Willen—
all of whom provided shelter and hospitality in
New York City many times over several years.
I could not have earned a living there without
their help. I am grateful, too, to Ulu Grosbard,
Mildred C. Swan, and my late sister Zaida Sutton
Swan for financial help at critical times. Finally,
I thank my editor, Robert Cowley, for encouraging
me to collect these poems.

Contents

Part One

THE
SOCIAL
CONTRACT

The Social Contract

God knows why you should pick on me
to save your soul from dissolution here.
But I have seen your forward grin become
a signal of distress as you attempt
to fathom what I, a stranger, make of you.

I shall, accordingly, provide a smile
which you may take to mean that we have met
and that I do, indeed, recall your face;
while I, in turn, interpret your relief
to mean that I am someone in your eyes.

Among Commuters

In the night in the train pulling out of the city,
standing in the swaying club car, drinking with others
whose faces are too familiar, whose names one does not
        want to know,
looking out of the grubby, pocked, three-star window
at the finale of a sunset, the long clouds the color of rust,
at rubble and tenement, at billboards that advertise space,
at space, one feels, or may feel, that at long last
one is escaping what?

Click of wheel assures you that you are leaving, leaving,
that on earth as in heaven flight is still possible,
that the half-seen faces staring from windows
        into the summer night,
enduring the noise of your elevated passing,
will slip from your mind even as they slip out of sight
like a drowning crowd in another forgettable movie,
that you can shed the daily skin of your existence
by being thus transported.

But the sun sinks and around you the faces flare,
ruddy as they celebrate once again the day's end,
the irresponsible interval between office and home,
between the pressure to produce and the pressure to relax,
to be attentive and loving: another man.
Through dark country now we move between our selves,
        as the train moves,
reluctantly, as if it had too often
reached its destination.

At the Suburban Station

The men are still laughing as the train slows.
Then they put their hats on.
Their hats cast shadows over smiling faces.

Down the long aisle the men shuffle slowly
to a heavy door
which each holds open for the one behind.

I watch a succession of hands
reach out, hold for a moment,
then slip away.

I think of the long step down
into the wifely night
that welcomes each man home.

The Mistress' Farewell

You must have grown up in rows somewhere—
rows of houses, rows of corn.
I don't remember and I don't care.
I call you a parallel man.
Run along now. That's a dear.

Anyway, don't just stand there
waiting to give me the cue
which way to move on now, love.
You're great at showing the way
when it's headed straight for infinity
but this skin's hard-pressed clay,
remember? You ought to.
You've had enough proof
night after night and day.
Take this then as my farewell letter.
Dear, I've taken a turn for the better
you couldn't follow for the life of you.

Good grief, though, don't think for a minute I don't agree
everything's impossible,
above all that . . . that *thing*,
that "really enduring . . ."
that "between us still
as thrilling when we're married and forty
or sixty as now"—a now that soon needed a date
safely past before it seemed fit to celebrate.
Face up. Admit.
We lived in a trumped-up memory
of what we had been or one day would be.
We were always too late
or too early.

For my part, love, I admit
to being so full of holes I
might just as well be sky
and done with it.
Of course you were right.
All your warnings sank in.
I just wasn't made, wasn't cut out
to be another pretty dumb broad
plugged into two eyes and trailing a cord
around the sheer hell of a home
you could come back to at night
to find neat as a pin.
Right. Right. I would have been "pure bitch,
distilled" as a housewife.
In spite of which,
you know as I do, we could have gone on,
estranged growing stranger,
much longer and faster,
if it hadn't been for. . . .
Under your particular knife,
love,
I've simply lived long enough.

I know what you'll say:
that I always had it in me
to be what I'm fast becoming;
that that was one basic reason
for "that thing's" impossibility;
that I was unstable at heart,
a woman for every damn season,
not just for that one that gave us our start
and which, with your great first gallantry,
you insisted I was and, being, should stay:
one spring, juicy spring, your spring.

For a whole month, remember,
we had flowers coming out of our ears.
You yawned cuckoos—
the only clock working.
There was no stopping us then.
We could have broken pavement
with our little toes, like the trees.
We taught that May how to spring.

Now, by my watch, it's fall.

Jesus!
Should I have done . . .
should I have gradually hardened
and sharpened as you did,
faced with, denying, our loss?
I've never told you this.
You know how I saw you
once in a dream—
you of all people?
A Protestant steeple,
a fine white moral erection asserting its pride
as it thinned to a needle
above a dying New England countryside,
then took up its cross
in thin air, like a good pilgrim.
Perhaps I should have
hardened and sharpened as you did,
only in me it struck a fear deeply
to see one so busily living,
so dutifully working at loving,
so busily loving though dead.

Fall is a season, too.
Everything comes down then.
I watch it all with an incurious
impersonality that takes over me like dirt.
I take on all comers.
For all their stabbing agitation
they leave me somehow untouched.
These great earthmovers move me frankly far less
than minor events like rain,
a breath of the sea blown in.
I stare up at the sky,
allowing all animals their pitiful death.
I feel like a planet.
My bones are full of stories told by bodies forgotten.
None seem funny or very important.
When I've forgotten I'm living, I listen.
I remember one now of an old man, bent,
walking my ridges. He carried a staff.
It must have been ages ago.
As he walked, aging and lost,
on my body, he pounded and cried
Let me in, Let me in,
and I did and he died.

I do not believe in the resurrection.
But we shall meet.
I shall not recognize you then.
I shall simply mother your rot
like a child who will not be born
the same again.

Refrain

You speak my own language.
I no longer believe you.
And silence is no way out.

Behind the smile we share
opens the hole in the face
of a man we shall never meet,
of a woman who picked the wrong time to run.

We speak the same language
they do not understand.
It fails to grasp. It is all we have,
except for our still demanding bodies.

Our eloquence lies in flesh:
skin warming to touch.
Their eloquence lies
in bones going nowhere.
We lie, they lie, eloquently.

You speak my own language.
I no longer believe you.
And silence is no way out.

Inaugural: An Anglo-Saxon Riddle

If the thin-skinned wince,
so be it. I myself was weak once.
Now let the dun field be seized, as in glass.

Locked up in its drop,
safely, no bud now will stir or burst.
Growth is a string of small detonations.
Spring, blowing its victims up, destroys
what I hold in trust.

Look. There. Everything is so much simpler.
Stripped of the conundrum of their leaves,
great trees are mere stick.
In vertical black
against a stiff snow, they cut this rune:
We can all do with much less.

Also this good riddance:
Many agitated birds have gone.
Quarrels are not, to my ears, music. Let them
go squabble where it's hot and every
barber warbles as

he strops his razor—
whereas I seldom, if ever, need
raise my voice above its level of ice.

Logical Progression

To say that "power is deafness" would be extreme.
But to say that strength, unlike power,
still can hear,
even if with only one ear,
and can still bend with grace, would seem,
at least to me, just.

To say that "deafness is an attribute of power
essential to its maintenance"
must, I suppose,
sound to the powerful as false
(supposing they could hear)
as it rings true to me.

To say that "this deafness, this attribute of power
essential to its maintenance,
might yet be,
if not cured, gotten through to"
is to grow hoarse as
those in power detect a faint buzz.

But to say: "Deafness, being an attribute
of power essential to its maintenance,
at last allows
no other recourse than
open rebellion" is to find
that these deaf can hear

a pin drop, through a wall.

A Tale for the Longhouse

The Indians were brought low.
If height couldn't dizzy them
abasement knew how.
From sheer shame
they almost toppled to fall
the few inches left.
Some took Christ as a pill.
They hoped it would give them a lift
or at least steady feet
in a heaven more natural.
Others heard an old face repeat
tales from a past more hopeful
than the lean-to they squatted in.
They learned what a tribe could do.
They weren't bothered about sin
so much as dishonor. They grew
up from their heels and went out.
You can't keep them down now.
Where skyscrapers start to sprout
like no tree ever did—hollow
from the start—they arrive
in their second-hand cars and sign on.
They rivet and buck their way up, thrive
at a height angels view with concern
and wouldn't tread if you paid them.
Those braves got their feet back.
Like a tribe, though, you can't nail them
down in one spot for long. Attack
and withdrawal is still their strategy.
They hang on right up to the top
but may take off before the glassy
walls are all in to wall a new crop
of white-collars in. It's not money
they're after, or just enough—minus tax—
to get back to their woods and relax
before raiding the next doomed city.

Declension

Set out now to follow in foxpath,
his russet cunning, and find him
gone, the wolf long since,
driven by houses whose doors lock,
leaving for kenning of craft
this stolid dog
accustomed to your smell.

At Break of Day

Each waking face, reflecting its loss,
adds to the sum.
Below the burning shoulder of the dawn
the numbered shadows
stretch, rising to celebrate anew
this giant's downfall.

America (A Formal Elegy)

Where the excessive land ends
   Or begins in its hesitant islands,
      Slow to begin, foreseeing,
         Reluctant to conclude, pondering,

Rocks are resolute, the trees bent.
   In slight, considered sums
      Those islands shine and lie,
         The unbroken nation opening

Beyond them, frugal no longer,
   No longer reflective, in its own
      Undulant motion involved, between oceans
         Unfolding. Scarcely the coasts

Remember, or the harbors of stone,
   Our needy arrival. Each
      Left some portion behind,
         And journey alters the traveler.

Even the transported body
   Of God here is uneasy,
      As foreign as those who came
         In his name, their eyes locked.

Dear Christ, though the Devil
   Himself sports in the thickets,
      Shameless, here we will build
         Our kingdom of light on earth!

They dared, and briefly
   A light was constructed among them
      Who spoke of a sun and died
         In the shadow. These, though, dared.

■

Meanwhile, inexactly we perish.
   In formal clothing and a stretch
      Of bone, our furious dreams
         Lie underfoot, fitfully

Withdrawn. Death as a stranger
   Comes, age as an enemy.
      Long lay silent to expand,
         Long buried, the plains,

And the marvelous slopes recall
   Seas gone, their fall,
      The grave, harmonious hills
         Relinquished, one by one.

What deed can fulfill
   Such dimensions of desire?
      Therefore leisure is large, pleasure
         Infrequent. The continent exceeds,

Through which, restless as rivers,
   We stray, mingle, descending.
      And after what far way wandering,
         To abruptly widen and be done!

The cities have been visited. The land
   Remains, as alien as the sea,
      As broad. And the singular islands,
         Aloof. They meet and leave us.

Fortune

You must know where they lead
Keep your hand to yourself

I shall not read either
those lines in your forehead

The spiders of anxiety
hunting your palm
the worms of anxiety
at work in your brow
they weave and burrow
ways to extinction

There is nothing there
There is nothing in that
for you

while the farmer goes
on planting his eyes
planting his hands and
when he is done
will sleep for a season
likewise

You worry too much
Don't worry
The body that rose
is not yours

Old Man Descending

It hurts to walk down these steps.
It will take a younger man's feet
to get up them again.
Fool! He will recognize
nothing.

Father, Father, Son and Son

Sweet father   I have shrunk a bit
I think   I know
although I think you see me grow
and so I do
although although
sweet father

I can tell when it began
Before I was a full grown man
I was a child   the child was
and then I thought and now I know
and so apparently I grow
sweet father

How far to go   How far to go
All clocks agreed the child ran slow
and so it did   a little man
before the hours began to know
the time before a cock could crow
or I woke up   sweet father

Before the hours began to know
I ran easily if slow
according to the clock   and still outran it
which left me large   which made you small
I saw you ticking on a wall
stricken with time   sweet father

I learned the minutes pain by pain
I saw them pass and come again
I watched how fear wound up and struck
I learned what discipline it took
to tick   You could not falter
on your wall   sweet father

You could not falter on your wall
With steady hands you measured out
the world on which all clocks agreed
that bound and rounded every sense
into the fixed circumference
of time and need   sweet father

When I was large and you were small
I still had room inside one head
for any other world instead
of one   the one on which all clocks agree
the one that I have grown to see
outgrow me in our time   sweet father

It grew in me with time until
what was inside and once a part
outgrew me and stood out
locked and common under a vault of sky
that shall not open
while the habitual clock it ticks in me

It ticks   I measure now what I can see
who see you leaving time behind
sweet father I would stop
to see you in eternity
but my enormous children crawl
I must not falter on my wall

Parabola

Children
barefoot
see rain patter up
to the soles of their faces
in a puddle's two spaces.

Even the most modern children
(under six) live before Newton,
who well knew how things fall
if not how time bends.

Lacking his fixed sense of gravity,
they still rise to every occasion
differently than we have every
better reason to expect.

While your shod elders regard stars
with a dim sense of personal loss,
the kingdom of heaven has not
yet been put out in you,
barefoot
children.

Still Life

Few homes are meant to be lived in long
But there   still
at the head of the table
my father the fog unfolds his napkin
My mother the wren
unties her apron

Able to hop and flop
unable to fly
we brood openmouthed
at the tale
of a meal
Food
gives way
to twitter and mist

Brother   Sister
Look over the edge of the nest
I dare you

Mab

A landscape hung with the laundry
of the newly dead.
I am no longer young,
but you?   A crone, her thick legs red
with the cold, stands
bent above a tub, scrubbing at a skin
like mad.   Her mouth
is full of clothespins, her hair,
once honey-colored,
now thin and white as snow.   When,
twisting out the one she's done,
she hangs it up to dry,
the line she pegs it on to flap its arms
and legs against the winter sky
is taut gut.   Oh, how the flayed things flap!
Angry new-born babies screaming to be fed.
Stomping across the frozen mud,
she heads back to her shack,
brushes two weathered hides aside
that serve her for a door,
then picks another body up
to plunge it in the steam.
Holding the nape so hard
that her knuckles bulge out white,
she whacks it against the board,
then scrubs the dead man out.
She wrings out each last dream,
then hangs him up to dry,
another wind-flapped baby
screaming to be fed. I touch
this crone, who turns,
who asks me to lie down,
who whispers who I am,
who kisses shut each eye.

Your work, my love, is never done,
nor will you ever die.

The Return

Turning from the holy example of saints
Crumbling into their contradictions
Our nakedness is new

Who discover rest
In this peace   bones over bones
Like hands on a chest

■

Without you I would not be who I am
Within you death smiles and cries
Like an old baby

While the song of all skeletons
Dressed or undressed   has become
Love buries us in time

Taking the Plunge

(For Hart Crane: born in Garrettsville, Ohio, 1899; lost at sea, 1932)

At six sharp the machines stop
that cool air in midtown cells,
easing the way through thin walls
for·heat stored in stone facing.
Let down, droves push
into the glittering oven
of an August night going full blast,
the sun stuck over New Jersey.
Unreal scenery above: a jet
moving up Fifth;
white breast, head of soot,
gull scanning clogged traffic.
Red switches to green:
permit me voyage, Crane.

Curt twang of bowstring,
the smack of the ax into the king's heart,
ring of pick against rock,
or even urbane maddening chatter of drill,
to each deed its native music,
while only now, overhead,
does its roar catch up
to where the jet was.
Innocence lies in distance.
Gulls and poets
stick by their squawk.

Some, though,
I among them,
fishing for change,
step down a hole,
stand hot in ragged file
waiting for doors to open,
sidle to sit disconsolate,

black thumbs
approving a newspaper.
(Vikings Discover America!)
Or doze, slumped,
the day's mask hung on a nail.
Some dive.
Wearing pajamas at noon,
he walks rapidly aft,
climbs up on the rail
("Thank God the sea is near,
that's all I can be grateful for")
jumps and goes under.

Horizon tilts,
slips under the wave.
Time, taut, runs out,
the loosened halyard, coming about.
Now skip the man
and praise the craft
of discovery, poem or ship,
launched in, outriding time.
Lashed to the ribs with spruce root,
free of the keel, strakes give,
gunwales twist in head seas.
Built to yield without breaking,
to speed well—supple, fabulous animal.
Sow, boar, man, fish,
leaf intertwine
in the frieze carved
on the ship's stem.
Eyes that stare from the oak prow
raise no "villas the color of stale mayonnaise,"

gaze fixed upon
gray slope
of the next swell.
Fare well.
Below, red, orange, yellow
fade. Green darkens.
Blue blackens.
Plucked spectrum.
End of the rainbow.

On Dive No. 30, Dr. Beebe reported
pale-blue lights close to the porthole,
three inches of silver, a rose-red flash.
Descending to depths of seventy-two-hundred feet,
he "collected 115,747 individual fish,"
96 percent of his catch luminescent.
Lord, to shine under such pressure
is next to divine!
And we feared to go under
in Midwestern cities.

Part Two

A
DOOR
TO
THE
FOREST

Fall

A door to the forest swings on hinges
as the invisible phoebe sings.
The floor is a roof fallen in.

Through arches of silence between,
a fox and a rabbit look out
for a clump or thicket of scent.

Listening, a man stands still as a tree,
a gun prolonging his shadow.

Only the blacksnake fully appears,
deaf and warm on a rock in the sun.

Common Prayer

Crows thrown in a light sky, leaving the air
Caw-riddled where they fly, turn in a black patch
Over the valley, switch to a shadow
On the hill where the yellow larches march

Between sharp fir and delicate willow.
Although it is autumn there is no mist
In the evening. The air is sharp as frost
Against which leaves fall and a hill stands out.

It draws a clear but casual distinction
Between this earth and that sky. Crows fit in
While, slowly, eels twist down to breed again,
Leaving their holes by some remembered stone.

After quick spring and a long summer,
Grass is dun and the trees' skeleton
Stands strict against the sun in the west—
Not giving up but gathering the ghost.

The blue is very blue against which these
Top limbs, top branches slip lightly up.
Edge and crown of the hill stretch with them.
Trees, of a still white fire, leap at the rim.

On Forgetting To Buy a Newspaper
the Day Before Yesterday

I turned with relief
to the leaves of this tree.

No wren edits
the oriole's repetitious report.

All news is of note,
sung.

Translate the chickadee's
two to read:

See! See!
Yet feel I fail, fail.

These Chinese will
not let me through their Wall.

But with what cheer
this. . . .   Nothing. Gone.

Instead, eclectic
catbird's gray miaow

grins familiar
from the tree: That's All,

Folks.   Oh Chinese,
translate me!

And with what cheer
this cardinal catches fire

while the goldfinch:
Look!   Ha!

I wear the sun
on my back.

Crow: And I the night
by broad daylight,

and you?
What?   Yesterday.   Tomorrow.

Then silence
dropped its spider,

and still each web I see
reminds me.

A Flock of Grackles

Grackles in a flock attract,
deserve, attention as they pract-
ice in mid-September,
limber-
ing up and up, black on black,
for the upcoming trek,
trying the sky
out; like a new cloud, busily improvising a shape to fly
in. Major shake-ups,
from top to bottom, irregularly occur
as the flock swoops,
scrambling the elements: Without demur,
the president steps down, his slot
instantly filled by a hip,
flip,
anonymous hotshot,
a flying fool
fresh from a stint in the secretarial pool.
Entire cabinets resign without slackening pace
or otherwise showing a trace
of resentment. Here, the fast shuffle
doesn't ruffle
a feather. Politics is not for the birds.

Netherlands' Birdscape

Warm as loaves in the magpied fields
rise the tan haystacks under the sun—
     nature with an air of the kitchen.

A stack of gulls drops in from the sea
that clips the modest living room. Pigeons
     peck pavement in the one big city.

Far from the homely wound-up ducks
hungrily waddling from nursery to pantry,
     the heron sticks to a ditch.

Will he pick up his stilts and be off,
when the last unschooled flash is billed,
     for a fresh lack of a home?

While no other notes have broken their bars,
swallows are privately slipping from wires
     stuffed with doubled Dutch voices.

People and Bats

don't mix. These light mice
that have learned to fly
at the price
of being blinded for life wake
an old fear. The quick
duck of the head, hands covering hair,
is instinctive. Even by broad day, the sight
of clawed wings stuck
upside down on a wall
can make our thin skin crawl.

Night
brings them flapping out of hiding
like bad dreams. Like fear.
Like this fear
that far overhead, beyond
the known sky,
something blind
and unmanned
we cannot see or stop
already drones or is silently gliding.

They dip
and swerve, guided by squeak
and ear. Their erratic
flight
resembles that of the butterfly.
Bat, *chauve-souris, Fledermaus,*
there is something freak-
ish about them as there
is about us,
who alone among primates walk upright.

Splitting Wood

You'll sweat, but it's a luxury.
The feel of the ax in your hand.
The curve where you grip it.
The way the thing rests, balanced
but with a heavy head
that's weightless only when it's swung.

Pick out a small log for a start.
One smack, they fly in two,
to lie there white-faced in the grass.

It's with the big ones,
where the blade gets stuck
so that you have to lift your ax
with the fat log still married
to your blade and turn
the ax around and shoulder it
and—clop—with any luck
split the wood wide open
that you feel included in the act.

The halves sail off,
leaving the freed blade
gazing straight up at some
invisible line
between your eyes.
And you feel, for a time,
the lightness of swung wood.

Heaven and Earth

(For Andrew Ritchie: 1907–1978)

It was a circle when I heard it first,
mid-March, about ten years ago,
of songbirds, lost,
I thought, circling in confusion in the night.
The sky was overcast.
I couldn't see a single star.

I stood there, face up, following the sound,
my head circling like the birds,
around and around.
They must be thrushes, a flock of them, I thought,
too early, northbound,
and feeling, as I felt, the cold,

and excitedly conferring up there.
It was like standing in a bell.
Then they moved higher.
They are climbing, I thought, gaining altitude
before leaving the air
above me empty as a church.

It was then that, swung once more, the bell broke
and fell, ringing all around me
a new music,
the sound now as if each of the pieces sang,
liquid and ecstatic,
of unearthly generation.

It was, I thought then, the sound of heaven.
When it was over, the sky
silent again,
it seemed to me the dead had celebrated
overhead, and withdrawn,
not to return in my lifetime.

March proved me wrong. Snow fell but the same song
circled up through another night
and fell, ringing,
and often, waking to moonlight, I heard it
as winter turned to spring.
It had to be a single bird.

Now, ten years later, I have learned its name.
Each March I watch to see
the woodcock skim
the ground, turn and spiral up to build his bell,
then break it up and come
down through his music to the earth,

a very plain bird, plump, with a long bill,
useful for unearthing earthworms.

Idyll, with Siren

Between the cat's hopeful appearances, creeping through snow,
this tree-sparrow flock, these slate-colored juncoes
pick at the seed,
fly off, perch, flit back, feed, while
snow continues to fall at an angle.

As the cat, reappearing, cocks its head,
there's a rush for the branches,
a smart rapping of beaks against branches,
as if only normal after a meal.
Attentively ignored,
will the cat fade? It chooses to.
A siren goes off in the town below.

As a result, perhaps, two cardinals arrive—this flame and its shadow.
Crested, splendid, the male pitches his torch
among brown crisp clubs the oak holds onto,
tenacious as the rich.
His fire doesn't rub off. The pair descends,
picks at the seed,
flies off, perches, flits back, feeds, while
snow continues to fall at an angle.

As the cat, reappearing, cocks its head,
there's a rush for the branches,
a smart rapping of beaks against branches,
as if only normal after a meal.
Attentively ignored,
will the cat fade? It chooses not to.
The siren is silent in the town below.

As a result, perhaps, the cat is black.
She creeps, like smoke,
over deeper snow.

Omen

You will not even notice our departure.
The small, falling like plump leaves
among the fallen leaves,
will lie indistinguishable, each with his song
locked in his throat.
The large, unable to climb, to soar,
will invisibly die in their high places,
which only the few sure-footed among you could scale.
Only the tame, safe in your cages, will, for a time, survive.

We have, it would seem, outlived our purpose,
whose strokes in the sky taught you symbols
to preserve what you thought.
In those days, we seemed lines drawn by a wise god
as we flew, flocked,
presaging more than a change of season.
Each savior in turn had his holy bird,
his practical, heavenly messenger descending
to peck a seed from the ear or to seal some voice as divine.

We who announced the birth of each sun,
who once were, to the discoverer,
true sign of the unseen,
longed-for land ahead, now may announce no new thing
save this darkness
which we, at your bidding, must enter.
We fall, as pit-birds fell, silent.
Their silence was always clear warning to you to turn back.
But you, hacking at shadows, still fail to hear us though we cease to sing.

The Cardinal Is

in green trees   blood red
the pennant of desire hoisted
Yet this blaze doesn't threaten to spread

Yet green trees that stood still
appear now to ring and circle
this single flame of bright arrival

And each in contradiction
shows more red   grows more green
as woods   taking aim   move in on

Him wings will save   But for such men
no refuge is   nor any protection
Unless the fire   Unless the sun

Now or Then

We shall leave it all behind,
as the saint his riches,
without feeling abandoned.

We shall turn back to the small grass
at the bearded wheat's feet,
our ripening grandfather.

We shall consort with boulders hunched
in their fields like whipped men
afraid to look up again.

We shall come to terms with the birds
whose language was foreign
to what was left of our ears.

We shall lie beside still waters,
listening like mothers for
a sound from the yet unborn.

From the trees we shall learn how to
climb both ways, up and down,
with the same daring and care,

while from the grouse and the woodcock
we shall learn to be still,
more still, then invisible.

Circle, with Penguins

Large wings rush past my window too fast to see
the body they bear.
My flying children!
To have lived long enough to have flown
and to have given up flight.
To take one's turn in the circle of fathers.

The earth turns away from the sun. The long shadows spread out
    into the night
and in the woods the birds settle down for the night, their songs
    tapering off
into silence. Large wings rush past my window too fast to see the body
they bear into the dusk. Bats flit around the tops of the tall poplars
and once again I am amazed that mice should have learned how to fly
at the price of being blinded for life, and, even more, that these birds,
resting now, started out as reptiles, that their feathers were scales once.

The earth has turned away from the sun and my children turn
    in their beds,
already dreaming, flying perhaps, thanks to that most ancient nub
of the brain, the reptilian leftover which, each night, takes over,
and a procession of birds marches into my mind, one by one
removing their tall hats to stand silently, their hands at their sides,
as if at some formal occasion: the birth of a child,
the death of a man. They recognize me. I recognize them.

These are the Emperor penguins. They have lived long enough
        to have flown
and to have given up flight for a life in the sea. Each winter, however,
"we march inland over a landscape of ice to lay eggs which must never
touch ice, because they would freeze then. The fathers receive the egg
        on their feet.
Far from the fish-thick sea, they stand there, starving. The cold
        would kill you.
They form a circle, each taking turns shuffling into the warmer center
of the circle of fathers until, at last, the hatchling is born or is not born."

Large wings rush past my window too fast to see
the body they bear.
My flying children!
To have lived long enough to have flown
and to have given up flight.
To take one's turn in the circle of fathers.

By the Brook

Fish in the brook slip out of sight without seeming to move,
from light to shadow to nowhere,

and the clouds let go of each other's hands
and are lost from the sky,

and the women stand in the field in traditional black,
saying, "Where are our men? We have lost them,"

and the men stand in the field in traditional black,
saying, "Where are our women? We have lost them,"

like clouds that, having let go,
believe they have been left behind.

I shall step back from the brook
and the fish that have vanished
will edge back into the light,
and there will be an end to mourning.

The Wedding

Floating overhead like clouds
three women turn to one

Thunder shakes my house
as she lets down her hair

Metamorphosis

But why precisely now, when I say
for once what I mean
(considering where we are and what we've, after all, been)
do you change so abruptly,
your eyes taking on that . . . go gray, turn in, assume
an interior lustre that eludes me;
lead, like a dream, only in?
We were so . . . not so much easy . . . but open before.
Our eyes, clear windows; the view, frankly sensuous—no more.
And now, inside your windows, this room,
this room with curtains, with curtains blowing and an open door.

I'm a plain blunt man.
Really, I am. I simply said. . . . And now you're off somewhere.
I'm aware of that. But why this peculiar retreat into . . . hell,
once out *this* door there isn't even a street—
more like an alley . . . a back-alley at that that,
once past the sharp-glass-sharded wall,
turns its back on the city and into a path
nobody's, obviously, walked for a long time.
You can tell by the grass,
tell by the moss
scraped off by our feet
on our way in, on our way up,
like the short green hair over the lip
of the giant in the old tall tale so beautifully told,
in passing, had he shaved,
into these woods.

And now that we're this far—
well, what can I say?
At least I recognized that quick coiled way
out of the city—
but this?
Glum. Grim. Green.
And by the way
hoo-hoo
where the devil are you
in this underwater scene
where the only little lights run
overhead like specious river laughter
or trickle down in splotches, in a long lean stain,
and there's no single sun
to say everything's simple . . . imperfectly plain?

Where
        hoo
            are
                you?

Christ! Out and down in this ribald dark
all talk turns into owl-talk.
In another world, God knows, daylight stands corrected, saving time,
while you . . . you must be gathering darkness like mushrooms.
I can't see hide nor hair.
For the life of me, I'm not sure where
you are or I am either except,
possibly,
lost, or found too often to be strictly true.

I call. I call.
My voice turns into echoes of my voice
and when you answer, everything replies.
The stalking hemlocks talk in rows
and the sleek beeches splashed with shadows speak
more softly, softly, until your call has shrunk into a shrub
or the slow stones only murmur.
Then call again
and for a time my voices chase each other only
until your answer meets them
and all around the sounds of recognition ring,
the long woods echoing,
as if, if we are lost, we are together lost and one,
though calling out apart, alone,
before the linked sounds dim and sink
to lie at last as grave as shadows on this silent ground.

Then, ironically,
there you are . . . were all the time, I suppose,
while I stood rooted in the bark-dark subaqueous criss-cross
of leaves and limbs rather pleased, I admit,
to meet you completely if only figuratively
(the way the shade of a man will be)
there you are . . . were all the time, I suppose,
having gathered sufficient darkness unto at least yourself
to stand quite alone in that slight clearing ahead
with only an oaktree for company.
Odd, how in that otherwise sun-struck patch,
the light still refuses to touch you,
stretches but doesn't quite manage to reach you.
Odd. A man could lose his head,
I suppose, searching out the undoubtedly subtle whys and the
     wherefores.
And yet—as far as I can see—
it's only you, waiting for me
—with a somewhat somber smile, I might add—
in that clearing just ahead,

as dark as dark as you are naked,
waiting for me
by an oaktree.

After the windows,
after the door,
after the shadows
rising and sinking on the forest floor—
at last to arrive,
at last to enter,
at last to come in.

Ah, sweet sister, it's no wicker cage you're burning me up in
now.
Sheer skin! Skin!
What have I done?
Christ! You wouldn't treat a dog this way
unless you were as you damn well may be
pagan,
heathen,
Indian.
Squaw. Squaw.
Look at my ashes!
They're flapping up black now.
The wind stings. All wings.
Wings for a cinder. Thin air for a home.
Come. Come.
By my last burst lights, I see
you glow, glow, glow.
When I said what I did
how could I know. . . !

O
caw caw
Love a crow

Air

air as a song
air as an air
as what clouds do
not need to say

wordless weather
as airs the young
birds study leaves
for until fall

lets fall its rud-
dy alphabet
that leaves all un-
done things unsaid

air as she's sung
as when in spring
each tree bush we
who alone can

read dead letters
may May each leaf
in turn puts on
greener meaning

About the Author

JON SWAN was born in Sioux City, Iowa, and graduated from Oberlin College in 1950. He later worked with the American Friends Service Committee in the United States and Germany and taught at the Ecole d'Humanité, an international school in Switzerland. Following a summer acting job at the Gateway Theatre on Long Island, Mr. Swan joined the editorial staff of *The New Yorker*, where he remained four years.

His first book of poems, *Journeys and Return*, came out in 1960, and his poems have appeared in several magazines, among them *Antaeus, The Atlantic,* and *The New Yorker*. In the late sixties several of his one-act plays were performed off-Broadway, at the Eugene O'Neill Memorial Theatre, and by the Seattle Repertory Theatre. A book containing three of his plays was published in 1968.

Mr. Swan works as a translator (from Dutch and German), as a freelance writer, and as an editor. He lives with his Dutch wife, Marianne, and their three daughters in Clayton, Massachusetts.